Crochet for Beginners

The Complete Guide to Mastering Crochet in 24 Hours or Less!

Dianne Selton

© 2016

Dianne Selton Copyright © 2016

Table of Contents

Introduction

Do you want to crochet? Well you've come to the right place. Crocheting is simple, and it's increased in popularity in the recent years along with knitting. It's considered to be an old pastime, and it's now popular with a whole new generation of men and women. It's fun and easy to do, and it makes a wonderful hobby where you can create something unique, beautiful, and even a gift that you can give to others.

Don't worry if crocheting is new to you, with these clear and easy steps it'll be easy to crochet right away. The projects you find in this book are easy to complete after you've learned your most basic stitches. Every step is provided for you clearly and directly. There's always something that you can do with a little yarn and some time on your hands.

There's no limit to what you can do. Remember that crocheting can be added to your other projects as well. Even if you knit or sew. You can make fully crocheted items, including clothing once you get passed the beginner level, but you are also able to make smaller decorations. Keep in mind that the smaller your yarn, the finer the detail that you're going to get out of your project. If you're looking for a bigger item, it's okay to have bigger yarn. Daintier pieces will need daintier yarn, but the important part is taking that first step and remembering to practice.

A Little about Crochet

The best part of crocheting is that not many tools are actually needed. You just need to buy your crochet hooks and yarn of your choice. You'll learn more about yarn in the next chapter. Just remember that crochet hooks will come in different sizes, which are all based on diameters. When looking for crochet hook sizes, you'll need to look on the flat thumb area where your thumb rests.

The size will be stamped on this part and is usually around the middle of the crochet hook. You can even get hooks made out of different materials. You have wood, metal or plastic to choose from. Some even have handles that have softer areas to grip to increase your comfort for long hours spent crocheting. This is great if you have arthritis because it'll keep your hands from tiring as easily.

	USA	English	Metric
	14	6	0.60
	12	5	0.75
	10	4	1.00
	—	3	1.25
	6	2.5	1.50
	4	2	1.75
	B	14	2.00
	C	12	2.50
	D	11	3.00
	E	9	3.50
	F	8	4.00
	G	7	4.50
	H	6	5.00
	I	5	5.50
	J	4	6.00
	K	2	7.00
	—	1/0	8.00
	—	2/0	9.00
	P	3/0	10.00

You'll find the crochet hook sizes demonstrated above, and you'll use each size for different patterns. The size of the hook is important because it, along with the size yarn that you choose, will determine how big your stitch is. This is called the guage. This will be important in different patterns and projects. For a beginning size, you'll want 2mm to 8mm. If you're just starting, pick a size 4 or 5. Remember that sometimes hooks are labeled with letters as well that correspond with the mm sizing.

Other tools you'll need include your sewing basket. You don't want to have to walk all around the house to get everything that you need. You'll also want a pair of scissors. New scissors are usually best because you'll need them to be sharp to cut yarn. Darning needles are best for sewing your finished project together. When looking for yarn, you'll find the number on its label as well. it'll tell you the weight, tension, as well as how you should wash it so that your finished project doesn't tear up or become pilled. Most yarn will even tell you what hook size is recommended. If you're trying to get yarn that matches, look for the dye lot number. This is usually on the band as well. this will make sure that you get the exact color and not just a slightly different hue.

A Little More about Hooks:

You already know that hooks come in a variety of materials, and aluminium hooks are considered to be the easiest to get ahold of and use. They will have a variety of width and sizes in the aluminum hooks, and you can usually find them at any craft store. They are very smooth.

Plastic hooks are a second favorite to many, as they are lightweight. Additionally, plastic hooks can be jumbo sizes as well. You may need a bigger size for larger projects.

Bamboo hooks are popular, but there is no added benefit. They're easier to break, as they are wood, but they are considered to be light and warm. These hooks are also available in a variety of sizes.

Steel hooks are commonly a small hook, and are used for when someone is crocheting fine threads. They are not needed for beginner crocheters. You may need them when you are working with crochet lace for doilies.

How to Hook Your Yarn:

If you're right handed, use your right hand. If you're left handed, use your left hand. This will be your hook hand, and your grip should be on the flattened part of the hook. Place it between your forefinger and your thumb.

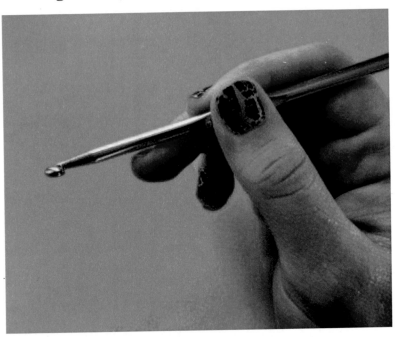

You'll hold it as if you would a pencil, and the hook should face down. Make sure that your fingers are placed roughly two inches from the tip. You'll see the proper way to hold the hook demonstrated above.

There is also the way of holding the hook vertical in your hand. Use whichever is most comfortable to you. Some prefer the vertical way as it allows you to grip the hook with your ring and pinky fingers and gives you more dexterity in your stitches.

Holding Your Yarn:

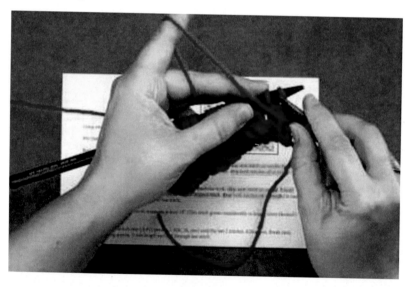

How you hold your yarn is also important if you want to crochet without hurting your hands. You need to control the yarn so that you aren't always trying to re-hook it. Tension is necessary to keep your stitches even and consistent, otherwise your pattern will show obvious flaws later on. There are multiple ways to hold it, but you should always start with the basic and adjust as necessary. The hand that you don't hold your hook with is your yarn hand. First, start by releasing yarn from the ball. Take your little finger, and wind it around it. It should be brought over your middle and index finger. You'll see someone crocheting with this method above. It's weaved around your fingers as shown above.

You use your forefinger to give the tension. The amount of yarn between your extended forefinger and your hook is the amount used for one stitch. This changes depending on the size of your hook and the type of stitch you are using.

Note: Make sure your hands are clean and DRY, this will make the yarn flow easier through your hand and allow for continuous work, versus stopping and starting.

A Little About Yarn

Yarn is the main material that everyone uses to crochet and you'll need it to create all of your pieces. You need to choose a yarn you like, but it's important to know what yarns are what and which are easier to work with versus others. You'll need to know if the yarn you choose is suitable for your equipment, and you'll need to know if you have what you need for whatever project you take on. If you don't know about yarn, this will seem impossible.

What to Look At:

You need to take certain aspects of yarn into consideration when you're buying it. The first thing you'll want to look for is texture. A smooth yarn will be easier to work with. So you'll want to pick this if you're just starting at crocheting. You'll soon be able to work with more difficult yarn, but choosing a rough yarn for your first pattern can leave you frustrated. It can also leave your hands in ruins as it will chafe.

Look for color as well. You may like darker colors, but when you're just starting, you'll want a lighter color. This is because in a lighter color you'll be able to see your stitches much easier. A darker color can hide your stitches, allowing for you to make a mistake much easier.

Always remember that yarn and crochet thread are not the same. You'll eventually be able to use crochet thread, but yarn is easier to work with. Crochet thread is considerably challenging, but it's good for daintier projects, such as doilies. You wouldn't want it for a blanket or scarf, though. However, you'll be able to use it for decorations, including bows and homemade buttons.

The yarn weight is actually important as well. Don't start with anything lower than a medium, but a higher weight will be easy to work with as well. If the yarn is too lightweight, you're more likely to make mistakes on your first few projects. Only move onto a lighter weight thread when you have had some experience and know your stitches well.

Types of Yarn:

You'll need to know what types of yarns are available as well, if you don't want to feel overwhelmed when shopping for yarn the first time. Wool yarn is extremely common, and when starting it is an excellent choice. It's easy to unravel again, and this allows you to rework it if you make a mistake.

You can also choose cotton yard, but you need to remember that it is inelastic, so it is more challenging than wool. You can use this for finer decorations, and it does make a great blanket and scarf.

If you're looking for a more affordable yarn, then there are acrylic yarns. They are incredibly popular due to the large array of colors. Are probably the most commonly used types in crocheting? They wash well, are easy to work with, do not chafe at the hands, and are good for avoiding issues with allergies and such.

If you are just starting, acrylic is the best to work with because it will not fray as much, it won't be a waste of money if you have to take it out repeatedly and will allow you to work on larger projects.

Starting with a Slip Knot

You'll begin all crochet work with a slip knot. It acts as the first stich that you make as well as an anchor point so that your yarn doesn't unravel as you work. You can tighten or loosen this knot rather easily, making it versatile. You'll need to follow the steps as seen below.

Slipknot

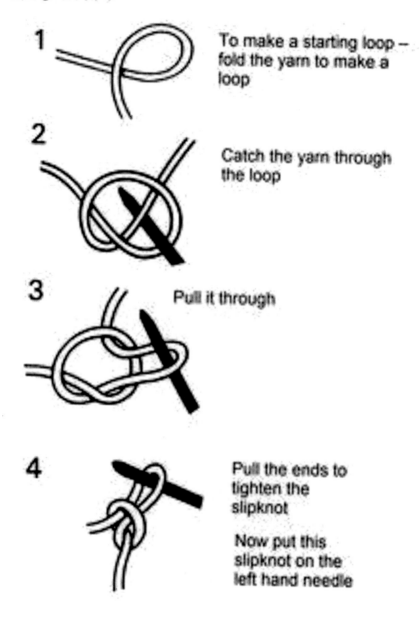

1 To make a starting loop – fold the yarn to make a loop

2 Catch the yarn through the loop

3 Pull it through

4 Pull the ends to tighten the slipknot

Now put this slipknot on the left hand needle

The First Step demonstrates making the loop. Place it fifteen centimeters (3 inches) from the end of the yarn to make sure that you have enough room. You want to make sure you have a long enough tail that you can weave it in later with a darning needle. If it is too short, you will not be able to do that and your project can unravel. Better too long, than too short.

Second, you'll pull in the end of the yarn that you're working with. The working end is what leads to the rest of your yarn. Pull it through your loop.

In Step Three, you'll have a slip knot created, and in Step Four you'll slip your hook through the loop, pulling on both ends of the yarn. This will tighten it. Don't tighten it to the point that it doesn't move freely down your hook. If it's that tight, then it's too tight. You want a loop that is slightly larger than your hook for ease in sliding. It should not be bigger than the thumb area of your hook.

With your slip knot created, you can move on.

Learning a Chain Stitch

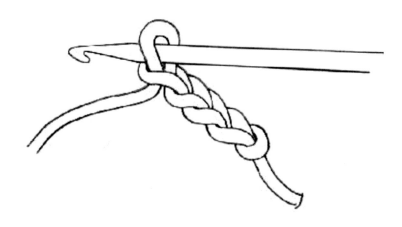

Your chain stitch is key to learn as it forms the foundation of any project your start. After learning your slip knot, the chain stitch looks like a chain of slip knots. It's really that simple, and you'll see it above.

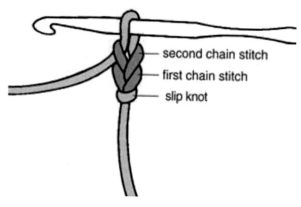

second chain stitch
first chain stitch
slip knot

Above, you'll see that the chain stitch moves upward from the slip knot. It's tightened into a beginning knot. You'll be using yarn over hook to create these stitches.

Yarn Over Hook:

Think of crocheting as numerous loops stacked on top of each other. One loop will need to be pulled through the next. Your loop will stay on the hook, and you need to keep it facing down. This helps you to catch the yarn. The yarn will then need to be brought over the hook again. This is demonstrated in step one. You'll see it's repeated in step three to create another loop. The term Yarn Over is often abbreviated as YO in many patterns.

Chain Stitch Steps:

Step 1: Your hands should always be in the starting position with the slip knot still on your hook. Starting position is your yarn hand holding the yarn at flowing tension and your hook hand holding your hook.

Step 2: Use the YO, pulling through to create your first chain.

Step 3: To keep it from coming undone, pinch it gently and repeat the first two steps. Continue until you have the right number of chains for your pattern or the length of the item you wish to create.

Double Crochet Stitch

$$\mathsf{T}$$

This is the symbol for the Double crochet stitch, abbreviated as DC in most patterns. It is simple to do and require you to work with the chain you just created. Each chain is considered an individual stitch to be worked with.

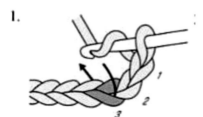

When you start, make sure it looks like the position above.

To start, you'll insert your hook into the second stitch from it. This will bend it upward into a 'V'. Now use the yarn over step and then pull your yarn through the previously created chain. Now you have two loops on your crochet needle.

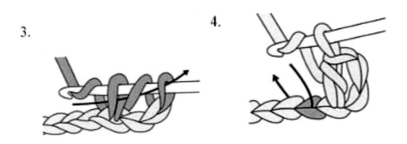

Use yarn over hook again, pulling it through both of your stitches. You'll see these steps above.

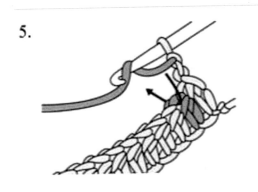

You'll continue by repeating and going along this pattern to make another row, as seen above. To do this, this will be where you turn, referred to as such in patterns.

Here you turn your work around, and then you're positioned properly for the next row. It's as simple as flipping your work over so that your previous row stretches away from your hook in the opposie direction.

To continue, insert the hook under your two threads at the top of the next stitch. Continue with the stitch you just learned, the double crochet stitch, until you're at the end again. Make sure that you check your number of stitches to match your pattern. If you're not used to it, it's easy to miss that last stitch. If you do, your pattern will start to get smaller with each row.

You can continue and make an entire project with this stich alone or follow a pattern to make more intricate designs.

A Half Treble & Treble Crochet

The double crochet stitch (abbreviated as DC or HDC) is dense, but this one is a little looser. It makes it softer, which is great when you're making accessories and clothing, especially for young children. It's represented in a patch above.

Step 1: Your yarn will need wrapped in yarn over. Insert the hook into the third chain. Use yarn over again, and pull it through.

Step 2: Now you should have three loops on your hook.

Step 3: Yarn over again, and then pull through to hook all three stitches. This should create one loop, and you've just completed your first half treble stitch. Continue until you hit the end. You'll need to make a turning chain when you get to the end. It'll be represented as ch 2 for chain 2. When your work is turned around, then you're ready to start a new row.

The Treble Stitch:

It's easy to start, and it's a little wider. You'll see the double crochet stitch demonstrated above, as well as the symbol.

Step 1: Start with yarn over, and then insert the hook. Do so on the fourth chain from the end of the hook. Use yarn over hook again, and pull it through.

Step 2: You should have three loops on your hook. Use yarn over again, pulling it through two of the loops. Do not pull through all three.

Step 3: You should have two loops on your hook, and now use yarn over hook again. Pull it through the two loops so you have one. This makes the first treble stitch. Keep going until you reach the end of the chain, and then use your turning chain stitch.

The Slip Stitch, Increasing & Decreasing

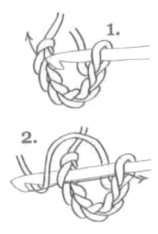

The basics of the slip stitch is seen above. It can be reduced into these two steps after you're used to it, but it's elaborated on below. As always, you'll start by placing the hook through the next stitch. Then use yarn over hook, pulling the yarn through the work as well as the original loop. This needs done at the same time. Your slip stitch is complete, as seen above.

About Increasing:

Different patterns will require you to create shapes in your crochet work. You'll want to increase and decrease to do so. This refers to the number of stitches that you have in your row. When increasing, work two to three stitches into the same stitch. The first stitch will be worked as normal, and then you insert your hook back into the stitch, and then create the second. The row will now be increased by one stitch by doing two.

The pattern will tell you how much to increase it. For example, you may see "tr3tog" this means treble crochet 3 together. "Dc" means double crochet.

About Decreasing:

Decreasing your number of stitches will also be needed for some projects. There is a basic way to decrease your stitches, and it shouldn't matter what type of stitch you're currently using. To decrease, take two or more stitches and crochet them together. Crocheting two stitches together will decrease it by one.

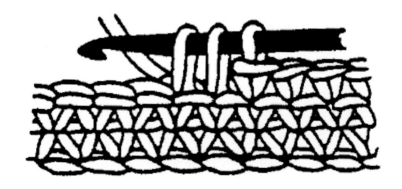

As seen above, you'll see three stitches that need to be worked together. Use yarn over, and then pull it through all three of the stitches seen. This should leave you with one loop on your hook.

Joining, Fastening & Sewing Yarn

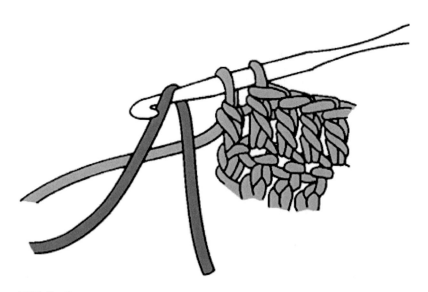

With larger projects, joining yarn is a necessity. One ball will not usually be enough, and joining yarn can be seen above. It doesn't matter if you're joining two colors to make your pattern a little more unique or joining another ball just because you've run out. You'll use the same technique either way. The change needs to be made at the beginning of a row. It shouldn't be done in the middle unless your pattern calls for it. This will normally not happen.

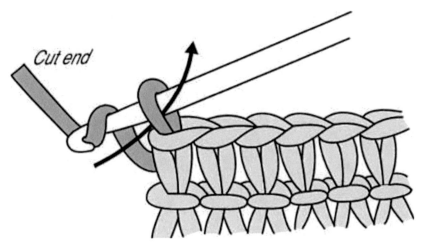

Step 1: You'll need to start by fastening your first color, as seen above. You'll then make a slip knot with the color or new ball of yarn. The hook still needs inserted in the very first stitch of that row. Slip the slip knot over the hook and pull it through.

Step 2: The new color has already been pulled through the stitch, and you'll need to do yarn over again to start a chain stitch. This helps to secure it, and then you can continue as if you didn't add in yarn.

How to Fasten It:

Your work could unravel if you do not fasten off the stitches that you are using, and it must be done correctly. To fasten your yarn, you'll have to start by cutting it. The tail should be about four inches long, so that you have length to weave it at the end. The loop should be loosened on your very last stitch, and the yarn that's been cut needs pulled through completely. Tighten it. Leave the yarn for now so that you can sew the item later.

Sewing in Crocheting:

When all the crocheting is done, in most projects, you'll have to sew the different parts together. The stitches that you use are usually hidden, giving it a purely crocheted look. This requires a tapestry needle which is also known as a large darning needle. You'll also need the same yarn to sew your pieces together to keep them hidden.

If you know sewing stitches already, then this is a much easier process. However, you'll need to learn the mattress stitch. It's the best and easiest way to sew your crocheted pieces together while making your sewing stitches invisible or nearly invisible. Your tapestry needle will need to be blunt. This will make sure that you do not pierce your yarn. You'll seen an example of the sewn pieces above. This is where the sewing is visible to make a pattern, which if commonly used in blankets and some scarves.

Step 1: Start on a flat surface and then lay the pieces next to each other. They should be side by side, and the inside should be facing up. This is commonly called the 'wrong side'. Your needle will need to be threaded with the same yarn, and then you'll secure it to the end of the work. Make a few stitches on top of one another.

Step 2: Take the first two edges of the stitches and pull them apart. You'll need to look closely to get it right. There are horizontal threads that connect them and you'll use these for the mattress stitch.

Step 3: Once they're pulled apart, your needle goes under them, and then you run it through the first and second stitch on the other piece. Pull your yarn completely through to create a mattress stitch.

Step 4: You'll then cross to the other piece again and this is following the same steps above. Keep going and you'll create a zig zagging pattern moving from one piece to the next.

Step 5: Remember that the yarn needs to be pulled tight each time a stitch is created. By pulling them tight, you are creating a seam that will keep your work held together properly. This is especially important if you plan on this being a heavy use item or washing it regularly. Once you've reached the end, you'll secure it with two to three stitches, depending on preference, on top of one another.

Buttons & Pom Poms for an Added Touch

In some designs, you'll need to sew on buttons, and it'll add an extra something to your crocheting. It doesn't have to be hard, and sewing on buttons can even be done by a complete beginner. You'll see one basic bather with buttons above, and these are often used for decorations. Buttons add a needed touch, especially when you're using what you've crocheted as a gift.

Step 1: Thread your needle with matching yarn to make it look more natural. You'll need to tie a knot at the furthest end. However, make sure the needle you're using fits through the holes of the button so that you don't need to cut it and transfer to a smaller needle. This will keep you from wasting thread or yarn, depending on what you're using. Once you've decided where your button needs to be, bring the needle up through the middle of the crocheted area. Bringing it from the rear and up to the 'right' side, which is the side you want to display. Otherwise, your button will be sewn on backwards.

Step 2:

You'll then sew two stiches on top of one another, and these stitches should remain small. This helps to secure the yarn or thread to the crocheted material. You do this before you try and sew the button on to make sure it'll stay securely. You'll see this above.

Step 3:

Next, you're going to take your button, placing it over the area that you've secured. Bring the needle up and through the hole on the button. The thread needs pulled all the way, and then you can push your needle through the next hole. Remember the thread needs pulled tautly each time. You'll need to do this four times. It may need to be done more if the button still feels wobbly. You'll see this above.

Step 4:

Flip it over and now you should be looking on the underside of the crocheted piece. This is where the button is already placed and you'll have to do two to three stitches, depending on preference, in order to tie the thread off. Cut the extra yarn or thread, as your button should now be secure. Make sure that you're careful with your scissor because if you cut your crocheted piece, you'll need to start over. It won't hold anymore.

Pom Poms:

Pom poms can be made in many different projects, and you can use them on bags, scarves hats, and even some blanket designs. You just need cardboard, yarn, and it's best to have round lids. If you don't have round lids, you can get a round shape that you can trace, and then you're ready to start.

Step 1: The first step is to decide how big you want your pom pom, and you'll want to find something similar to the size that you're looking for. Many people will use a jar lid, CD, or even a small bowl. Anythign circular will work, and then you'll want to place it on your cardboard. Take a circle and trace it. Next, you'll want to trace a smaller circle in the middle. You'll want to make two cardboard pieces that are shaped like doughnuts. They need to be identical.

Step 2: It's best to use a small ball of yarn, but you can use a large one as well. if your'e using a larger ball, you'll need to make a smaller ball out of it and cut it. You can also wind it over your figners instead of using cardboard, as seen above, but it will make a different pom pom.

Step 3:

In this step, as seen above, you'll place your discs together. You'll then start to wind the yarn around both discs.

Step 4:

Try to hold the two discs together, as you can see in the above picture, and then wind your yarn over it and threw the hole. Keep repeating until you have covered every bit of cardboard. You need to keep repeating this. You'll know when to stop when the hole is too small for you to pass any more yarn through it.

Step 5:

Next, you'll need to insert your scissors. To do this, you'll want to take one of the blades, and slide it between the two cardboard pieces. Cut through the yarn. Move the scissors completley around, cutting as you go. You should cut all the way around.

Step 6:

Pull the two discs apart and then wrap yarn between them. This ties the middle of your pom pom, and you'll need to make sure that you have a tight knot made to tie it. you'll want to repeat this process to make sure that your pom is truly secure. Clip the ends of your string or strings.

Step 7:

Cut the discs away or gently pull them off. This will leave you with a pom pom, as seen above. You can use this in your crochet projects.

Some Basic Terminology

Not every book will be as easy to read as this one. You now know the basics of crocheting, and you're ready to move on to something a little more complicated. Before you do though, you'll need to learn the numerous abbreviations that are used in these patterns so that you can read them correctly. These terms will be used in this book for the patterns as well, making sure that you get used to them to help you move forward.

The first thing to know is that the UK and the US do label stitches differently, so you'll need to know where it comes from if you want to understand your patterns properly. You'll find an easy conversion chart below.

UK		US	
Chain	Ch	Chain	Ch
Slip stitch	Ss	Slip stitch	Ss
Double crochet	Dc	Single crochet	SC
Half treble	Htc	Half double	Hdc
Treble	Tr	Double	Dc
Double treble	Dtr	Treble	Tr
Triple treble	Ttr	Double treble	Dtr

Skip a Stitch:

This means that you'll miss your next stitch. You will continue with the next one after the stitch that you've skipped.

Dc2tog:

This is an abbreviation that means you need to put two double crochet stitches together to form one stitch. To do this, you'll need to put your hook into the next stitch, and then perform yr (yarn over), and then draw it completely through. Don't finish the dc (double cross) stitch. The hook will then need to be put into the next stitch, yr, and then pulled completely through it. This will put three loops on your hook when done correctly, and then yr to pull them together.

Foundation Chain:

A foundation chain will be your base chain and you'll add stitches on top of it. This is what you'll work all of your following stitches back into.

Foundation Row:

This is a little different than a foundation chain, as it's the row that you're working into the foundation chain.

Turning Chain:

You've already learned how to turn a chain, and turning chain refers to the stitches that you're using as extras to work with at the beginning to create the new row. It'll bring you up to the proper height to start the next row. Different

repeat from...	
Double treble crochet (dtr)	Yarn over 3 times, insert hook the stitch or space indicated, pull up a loop (5 loops in hook), *yarn over, yarn over, pull yarn through 2 loops on hook; repeat from * 4 times.

myhappilyeverafted.com

○ CROCHET CHEAT SHEET VIA HAPPILY EVER AFTER CRAFTED

REPORT

You'll sound like an expert once you're learned the basic stitch terms and tips on this handy Crochet Cheat Sheet! It shows the full stitch name plus the abbreviation used for the stitch on most patterns and also how to make the stitch.

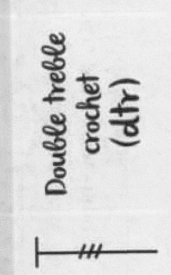

WHAT OTHERS ARE READING

Crochet Troll Doll Best Patterns

Wash Cloth Puppies Quick Video Tutorial

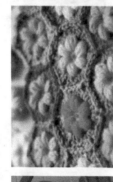

Daisy Puffagons Crochet Tutorial Watch The Video

Granny Square Crochet Bag Free Pattern

19 Mile Lys r
18 Mile Jumen

17161 ALVA Rd
SD CA 92127

Cheat Sheet

	Stitch	Instructions
	... stitch (ch)	Yarn over, pull yarn through stitch on hook.
•	Slip stitch (slip st)	Insert hook into stitch or space indicated, yarn over, pull yarn through loops on hook.
+	Single crochet (sc)	Insert hook into stitch or space indicated, yarn over, pull up a loop (2 loops in hook), yarn over, pull yarn through both loops on hook.
T	Half double crochet (hdc)	Yarn over, insert hook into stitch or space indicated, pull up a loop (3 loops in hook), yarn over, pull yarn through loops on hook.
T	Double crochet (dc)	Yarn over, insert hook into stitch or space indicated, pull up a loop (3 loops in hook), *yarn over, pull yarn through 2 loops on hook; repeat from * once more.
T	...	Yarn over twice, insert hook into stitch or space indicated, pull up a...

... stitch ...through 2 loops on hook...
...loops on hook, * 2 times.

$$\frac{75}{\frac{3}{4}1}$$

stitches can require different numbers of these stitches to work properly.

Dc3tog:

This is commonly called the cluster stitch. This is where you work three of your dc stitches into one, and you'll be working with the three stitches in a row, but it'll result in four loops being on your hook. Yr, drawing it through all four.

Acrylic: This is a synthetic yarn, which is why it is more affordable.

Black Loop Only: This is where you'll focus only on the back loops that you are making.

Back Loop SC (Single Crochet): This is another variation of a SC stitch, which will focus on just the back loops when making it.

Color Flashing: This is seen in many patterns, and it's an effect that happens if you're using a variated yarn. You'll have unintentional patterns show up in your work, which will create unique patterns.

Coned Yarn: This is a yarn that has been wound onto a holder that is cone shaped, and it's often easier to work with as you move on to more complex patterns.

Floats: When crocheting, there is some unused pieces of yarn, or rather strands that will be carried onto the back of the project.

Frog: This is used as a verb in crocheting, such as "to frog". It is to rip out your stitches. This will add decorative or functional pieces. This can be used for when you're adding buttons.

Freeform Crochet: This is where you aren't crocheting from a pattern, and this is great when you're practicing your stitches. You explore the craft, and you'll usually end up with a unique pattern.

Granny Square: This is a crochet pattern that is just made of a simple ring of chain stitches, and then you build on it outward. They are often put together to make a blanket.

Inelastic: When you're working with an inelastic yarn it won't recover its original shape quickly if at all after you've stretched it.

Kitchen Cotton: When you're looking for a yarn that's easy to use and useful in projects, you'll want to find a kitchen cotton. You can use it for placemats, potholders, and even dishcloths.

Pjoning: Once you know how to use an ss (slip stitch) easily, you'll be able to move on to a pjoning, which is where you use it to create different, unique fabrics.

Plarn: You'll find this when you're shopping for yarn, as it's a plastic yarn. It's often recycled, where bags and other plastic items were cut up and repurposed.

Place Maker: You'll want to use these when you're having to stop a project, and it's where you mark it in a way that you can remove later so that you don't lose your stitch. Many people will use safety pins that can easily be taken out.

Protein Fiber: This is a fiber made from protein, but it's not something a beginner should be using.

Scrapghan: This is where you make an afghan, which can be put together through granny squares or granny triangles, but you use your yarn Scraps to make it. This will often have a large variety of colors and yarn types.

Shell Stitch: You'll learn this as one of your last stitches in this book, and it's where you've looped multiple stitches into a single one.

Tapestry Needle: This is a sewing needle that is often used in embroidery.

Variated Yarn: This is a yarn that has a variety of colors, allowing for unintentional patterns of color to appear in your pattern.

Self-Striping Yarn: This is a type of variated yarn, and it has two or more colors in it. It usually does not change colors quickly, so you'll have long stretches of each color. You can get some variegated thread that has a shorter stretch of each color.

Work Even: This is your goal with most patterns, especially as a beginner. You'll want to continue in the same stitch pattern. You do not want to increase or decrease.

Worsted Weight Yarn: You'll find this in many simple patterns, and it just means a medium weight.

Yarn Cake: This is a method that you use to wind yarn.

Abbreviations:

Beg- beginning	Hdc- half double crochet	Sp(s) – space(s)
Bg- block	Htr – half treble crochet	St(s)- stitch(es)
Cc- contrst color	Inc- increase	Tog- together
Ch- chain	Rep- repeat	Tr—treble crochet
Dc- double crochet	Rnd- round	Tr tr- treble treble crochet
Dec- decrease	SC- single crochet	Ws- wrong side
Dtr- double treble crochet	Si st- slip stitch	Yo- yarn over
[ ] = work instructions within the brackets. Do this as directed		
( ) = work within the parentheses as the instructions direct you. It'll tell you how much to do so		
*= repeat what instructions followed the single astrix. Follow the directions		
**= repeat the instructions that followed the double asterisks, as directed and so on		

Refer to the chart above if you get lost trying to understand abbreviations in patterns and projects. Eventually, you will memorize them, but a chart is always helpful when you're just starting.

For an added benefit, you'll find a symbols chart below.

symbols	US crochet term	British crochet term
●	slip stitch	
○	chain stitch	
✕	single crochet	double crochet
+	single crochet	double crochet
T	half double crochet	half treble crochet
Ŧ	double crochet	treble crochet
X̃	crab stitch	
Ā	double crochet two together (dc2tog)	
V	2-hdc into same stitch	
V̄	2-dc into same stitch	
Φ	3-hdc cluster (bobble)	

Making Crochet Hairbows

Crochet hair bows are a great gift, and they're a great style. You'll be able to add buttons or pompoms if that's your choice, but you'll find that these bows are great on their own as well.

Ingredients:

1. Yarn (Choose Your Own Color)

2. Small Crochet Hook (No larger than a 6.5)

Directions:

1. If you want a smaller bow, your chain will be eleven stitches. For a larger sized bow, your chain will be 16 stitches.

2. Start with a SC in the second stitch from the hook. And continue with SC until the end. Then you'll use a turning chain.

3. Take chain one with a SC in the second stitch from your hook. You'll complete this until you turn, repeating it four more times. It'll be more if you want a larger bow.

4. You now need to assemble your bow, and to do this you'll start by folding it in half. You'll want to fold it lengthwise, and then take the matching yarn (or contrasting for a new look), and wrap it around the very middle of your crocheted bow. Make sure that you tie it off securely.

5. You will then want a hair clip if you plan to wear it in your hair. This is optional, as many people use these as decorations. You can wiggle the clip through the back of the wrapped portion of the bow. Other people glue these bows to barrettes to make sure they are secure. A hot glue gun is recommended.

Crochet a Triangle Piece

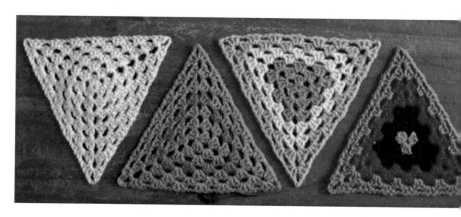

You may be wondering what the point of crocheting a trianagle is, but it's a great way to make a piece to sew together to create a blanket or scarf later on. You can easily turn them into unique squares and patterns, and it's an easy and safe way to manage your stiches for the first time. You'll learn to make different patterns in your triangles as well, as seen above. These will help to give you a more extravagent and detailed look to any piece that you're making. You can turn two of these into a pot holder as well.

Materials:

1. Hook #7

2. Yarn (Medium Thickness)

Directions 1:

1. Here you'll learn to start at the point, but you can also start at the base for a triangle. It all depends on your preference. You'll make a sk (slip knot) and then a ch (chain stitch).

2. Turn what you're working on and inc (increase) by a single stitch. Right at the beginning, and then d so at the end of each row. Keep repeating until you have the triangle as big as you want it, and then fasten it.

Directions 2:

1. In this set of directions you'll start at the base, and so essentially you'll be working backwards.

2. Your chain wil be 15, and then you'll dec (decrease) at the beginning as well as the end of every row. There will be two loops on yoru crochet hook, and you'll need to fasten them off.

A Simple Shell Blanket

For this chapter, you'll need to learn how to make a simple shell crochet stitch, but it's still compatible with any beginner who's practiced. You'll see a simple shell stitch above.

Step 1:

Start with a single color, and you can choose to add more lately if you desire to do so. You'll start by making a ch (chain), and you'll just use what multiple you prefer.

Step 2:

You'll need to work a SC (single crochet stitch) into the second ch (chain stitch). You'll judge this by where your hook is.

Step 3:

You'll then skip the next two ch (chain stitches), and then work a dc (double crochet stitch) into the next ch (chain stitch) afterwards.

Step 4:

Work in four more dc (double crochet) stitches into the same ch (chain stitch) for a total of five dc (double crochet) stitches.

Step 5:

You'll need to skip the next two ch (chain) stitches, and leave them undone. Then you'll make an ss (single stitch) into the next ch (chain) stitch after you've skipped the unworked ch (chain).

Step 6: Skip the next two chains, and you'll add five more dc (double crochet) stitches when going to the next chain stitch.

The Simple Shell Stitch Blanket:

Now that you know your simple shell stitch, you'll be able to practice on this quick and easy blanket. How big you make it is completely up to you, but make sure that you have enough yarn or are willing to change colors. Patterns usually come with practice, and then you'll be able to add and change colors whenever you want to, making everything you do a little more unique to your personal preferences.

Materials:

1. Size K Hook

2. Worsted Weight Yarn 5 Skeins (7 Ounces) to create a blanket of about 52x54"

Directions:

1. Your starting chain is a multiple of three and then add one. On your first row, SC (simple crochet) in the second ch (chain) from hook and SC to each of the stitches going all of the way across. Chain 3 turn.

2. Row 2: You'll skip your first two stitches, *3 DC (double crochet stitch) in the third stitch, skip the two stitches*, and then repeat * to * all the way across. You'll end with DC in las stitch CH 2 and then turn.

3. For Row 3: You'll skip the first stitch, then DC across the entire row, and then CH 3 and turn.

4. You'll then repeat both rows two and row three for the pattern, continue with this until it's the right length.

5. On your last row, which has to be after the row 2 pattern, chain stitch 1, and then turn. SC in the second stitch, and then follow the remaining stitches all the way across.

6. Bind off your stitches so that you can then weave in the ends.

Creating a Valentine's Day Heart

Creating a Valentine's Day heart only takes a beginner level skill, but you'll want to make a few. There's nothing like surprising your sweetheart with something that literally comes from the heart and is made with your hands. You can use any colors. Traditional or otherwise.

There is no limit to what you can do with these little hearts. When you get the basics down of what you're doing, you'll be able to adjust this pattern to make bigger or smaller hearts. Some people will even make two of different sizes, fastening them both together to create a unique Valentine's Day decoration.

Materials:

1. Worsted Weight Yarn

2. Size H Hook

3. Tapestry Needle

Instructions:

1. You'll be using a ch (chain) 7. SC (single crochet) the second chain, and go the rest of the way down the chain, use a ch (chain) 1. Then turn using a 6 SC (single chain).

2: On row two through three, use a SC (single chain) for each stitch, make a Ch (chain) 1. Turn 6 SC.

3: Now that you're on row 4, use a SC (single chain) in the first three stitches but no more, ch (chain) 1, turn 3 SC (single crochet).

4: For rows five through seven, you'll need to use a SC (single crochet) stitch for each stitch across, ch (chain 1) and turn 3 SC (single crochet).

5: As soon as you get to the last row, you'll want to continue to SC (single crochet) around the entire edge of the heart.

6: Once you reach the bottom stitch, this is where your slip knot is, do a SC (single crochet) then a ch (chain) 1 and then a SC (single crochet) all in one stitch.

7: When you're at the top of the "V" indent, you'll need to make a slip stitch instead of using a single crochet. Then join it and fasten it off.

Working with Double Strands & More

You won't always be working with a single strand, and there are some more complicated things that you'll need to learn before you move onto some of the beginning patterns to see what you can create. Don't forget that you can practice the stitches before starting a project, which will always make your project turn out a little better.

Working with Double Strands:

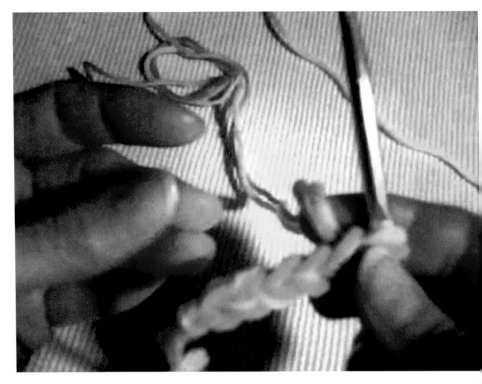

There will come a time when a pattern will ask that you work with two strands, and you'll do this at the same time. It can either be of the same color or of different colors. You'll have to use each strand together to create your slip knot, and then you'll continue like usual, treating it as if it was one strand. Make sure you keep them together.

Making a Cord:

You'll also need to learn to make a cord when crocheting before you start, and as seen above they can be turned into simple bracelets that you can even braid together later. There are different reasons that you'll make a cord, as you'll find out when creating your first patterns.

Step 1: You'll have to take two separate lengths of yarn, and then you'll want to double them over.

Step 2: Start by making a slip knot on the crochet hook, and this must be done with both pieces of the yarn.

Step 3: You're now ready to make the first stitch on your cord, and then you'll pull this first loop through your second one.

Step 4: You're now going to alternate your yarn, and then continue to pull the opposite one through the loop made from the other yarn onto your hook. The more you do, the more it'll start to resemble a cord.

Step 5: You're now ready to finish your cord by pulling one of the pieces of yarn through the opposite loop. Then pull it tight, securing it and teeing two knots for each strand of yarn.

Making a Ridge:

Making a ridge gives texture to your piece, and you'll see an example in the picture above. The main reasons that ridges are often crocheted is so that you can add a detail to a design, but it will also give a textured effect when you're using it to finish a design.

Step 1: Start by making your slip knot, and then create a foundation chain.

Step 2: You'll then add in a double crochet stitch, repating it along the row.

Step 3: You don't want to turn your work. Instead of turning, you'll work in a single crochet sttich all the way from left to right.

Step 4: Next, you'll need to make a slip stitch in your turn chain to make sure you end the row.

Step 5: You're now working on chain 3 stitches, and you'll have to skip the first stitch, making a double crochet stitch inside the back loop when put through the second stitch away from your hook.

Step 6: Just repeat until you get the desired ridge.

Creating a Shell Border:

You already know about a shell stitch, and you'll find that a shell border is a great touch to any design. When you know how to make a shell border properly, it's easy to add to any design and make your gift or project even more unique. Adding it in a different color, as seen above, gives it a new pattern as well.

Step 1: You'll need to start by making a slip knot, and then crochet your foundation chain. Next, work in a SC (single crochet stitch), into your second ch (chain) away from your hook.

Step 2: Skip your next two stitches, as you did in a shell stitch before, and then work in a dc (double crochet) stitch into the next chin.

Step 3: You'll need to make four more dc (double crochet) stitches, into the same ch (chain stitch).

Step 4: You'll then need to skip to ch (chain stitches), and work a SC (single crochet stitch) into the next chain after.

Step 5: Skip the next two ch (chain stitches) again, and you'll need to start again.

A Picot Stitch:

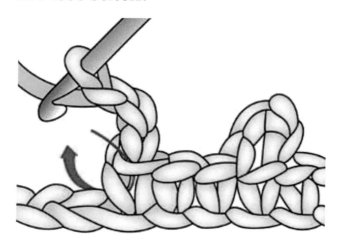

Picot

A Picot stich will also add a lot to even beginning crochet projects. This stitch is primarily an edging, so it's easily added in. You can add it to a blanket or a garment. You can even put it onto the edge of something that you've already created.

Step 1: Start with SC (single crochet stitch) then ch (chain stitch) 3 stitches across and a SC (single crochet stitch) into the next one.

Step 2: SC in the next three stitches.

Step 3: Ch 3 and SC in the stitch which will form your picot stitch.

Step 4: You'll then repeat both steps two and three. Do this until you reach the last stitch of your work to create the chain?

Making a Soap Saver Bag

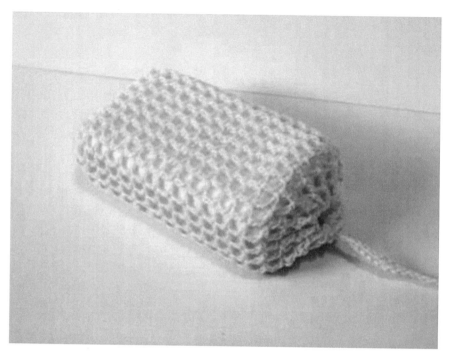

There's no reason to deal with those little bits of soap anymore. A soap saver is a great gift, and it's also a great addition to your bathroom. You can make them in different colors and patterns, but this one is simple and easy to do. It's a great project for even a beginner, and it'll help you to practice rounding. You can gauge how well you're doing because one inch should be three rows and four stitches.

Materials:

1. 5.5 mm Hook

2. 5.0 mm Hook

3. Cotton Yarn (one or two colors)

4. Yarn Needle

Directions:

1. Take your 5.5 mm hook. Make 11 ch (chains).

2. Row 1: Sc (single crochet) in the 2nd chain from your hook, and do so in each chain that goes across as well. This will give you 10 sc. Now, turn.

3. Row 2: Ch (chain) 1, sc (single crochet) in each stitch across. Now you have ten single crochets, and turn.

4. Row 3: You're now starting to make your bag. Start ch (chain) 1, and then 2 sc (single crochet) in the first stitch. In each stitch, single crochet. Do this until you get to the last stitch on that row, and then you'll need to make a 2 single crochet. This will be done in the last stitch on that particular row. Work three single crochets all the way down the side of each of the three rows. Go to your bottom loops from your first chain, and then do 2 single crochet in that chain. Then single crochet in each of your chains until you come to the last one. Next, make two single crochet stitches in the last one. Work three sc stitches up the side of the rows, joining in the first single chain. You are not going to turn because you've already

managed to keep your round shape. This should total to thirty stitches.

5. Row 4: Start by making 4 chains (dc with a sc). Then skip the next stitch *dc into the next stitch, ch 1 and skip the next stitch ** going in a circular shape. You'll then join them together at the top of the turning ch. It should make 15 dc stitches.

6. Round 5: Make 4 ch (dc with a sc), *dc in ch1, and then create a space with 1 ch ** Repeat from * to ** all the way around, joining the round at the very top that's at the end of the turning chain. There should be 15 dc stitches.

7. Rounds 6-9: You'll continue with the same pattern that you did in round 5.

8. Round 10: Make 1 ch, hdc (half double) in each chain. Leave 1 space and dc all the way around. You'll then need to cut the yarn, but remember to leave a tail. Join the tale using an invisible join. You'll need to thread the tail through the yarn needle, and then insert that needle under the last stitch. Pull it through. Next, place the needle and pull it through the chain of the next stitch. All of the tail should be inserted when you're done.

9. Drawstring: You now need your 5.0 hook, and you'll want to work a tight chain consisting of seventy chains. You'll then pull the yarn through the last chain. Don't forget to leave a tail. The tail will then need threaded through the needle, starting to

weave the drawstring. Knot both ends together, trimming the lose pieces. It's now ready to use.

A Simple Pot Holder

When beginning, it's best to always make something that you can use around the house or give as a gift. This will help you to have the drive to continue. One thing that you can use multiples of, is a pot holder. You can even make sets to give to someone using the same pattern or at least the same color of yarn with different patterns.

Materials:

1. Worsted Weight Yarn

2. 6 mm Hook

3. Tapestry Needle

Directions:

1. Start by crocheting 19 chains.

2. Row 1: Sc into the 2nd ch from your hook. *Sc into the next ch*. Now, repeat from * all the way across. Ch1, and then turn. When this is done you should have 18 stitches total.

3. Row 2: *Sc into the next stitch*. Repeat from *, going all the way across. Ch 1, and then turn. This will be another 18 stitches.

4. Repeat Row 2. You'll do this twenty times total. However, add more if you want a longer length. Do not fasten it off.

5. Ch 5 and make an ss (slip stitch) in the beginning stitch. This will form a loop.

6. Now, fasten off, weaving in the loose yarn.

A Little About Making Shapes

You're not just going to want to make triangles and squares and learning how to make shapes in crocheting is what will help you to expand from beginner projects or improve upon them. Just remember that all of your possibilities are endless. You'll want to practice your shapes if you want to get a good grip on your stitch skills.

Making a Circle:

Making a circle is important for many projects, including coasters and pot holders.

Step 1: Make a chain by six (Ch 6).

Step 2:

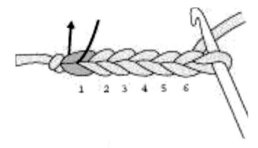

You'll then insert the hook into the first chain stitch, as seen above. This will form a ring.

Step 3:

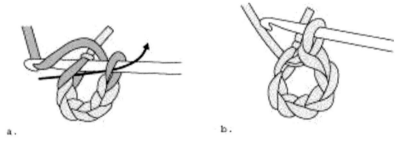

a.   b.

You'll then use yo, and then draw the yarn through that stitch. It will then be drawn through that loop, onto your hook. This completes your center, as seen above.

Step 4: You've made your previous round, but you'll work each stitch into it. Then work one stitch into the next stitch, then two into the next, all the way around. Make sure to end each round with a slip stitch.

Step 5: Then repeat step three until you get the desired size of circle.

How to Make a Square:

It's important that you practice making squares, as they are one of your most basic stitches when starting crocheting. You can do so much with squares, so they are a very versatile crochet skill. So let's go over it once more. Using variegated thread will make such a simple square have an involuntary pattern, which will create a one of a kind look when you sew these squares together, especially if the variegated thread is in different colors per square, creating some sort of pattern.

Step 1: Make a slip knot and then create the foundation chain.

Step 2: Then you'll make a half double crochet stitch.

Step 3: Create a SC (single crochet stitch) in each stitch that is on the rest of that row.

Step 4: Turn what you just made at the end of that row, and continue to repeat steps two and three.

Step 5: Repeat step 4, and keep doing this until you feel you've completed the desired size of square.

Using the Reverse Stitch

There are numerous stitches in crocheting the further you get along, but you'll find that there are also many stitches that you'll need to work in reverse or in different patterns. That's what this chapter is about, allowing you to branch out into even more patterns.

The Reverse Stitch:

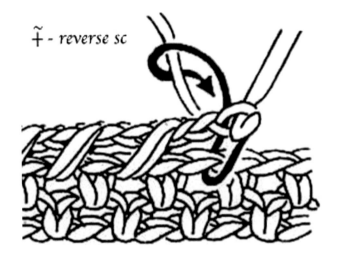

You'll see an example of the reverse stitch above. You'll also find that the reverse stitch is commonly called the crab stitch. This stitch will create a rounded and slightly twisted edge, and it's also a stitch that is used to finish a project.

Step 1:

You start by inserting your crochet hook from the front all the way to the back, and then into the stitch to the right. The right side of your work should be facing towards you.

Step 2:

Yr and then draw it through the stitch, and it needs to be drawn in similarly to a SC (single cross stitch). It's just done in reverse.

Step 3:

Yr and then draw it through the two loops that should be on your hook, which will complete the single reverse crochet stitch.

Crochet Tips for Beginners

As you continue to crochet, you're going to learn a thing or two, and you're going to learn how to make it a little easier. It doesn't matter if you do it in your spare time or if you do it to destress. The reasons won't make a difference, and everyone can improve. There's no reason to get frustrated, but when you're beginning, it's easy to. These tips will help you to keep crocheting and even get better at it.

Tip #1 Stretching

Crocheting can be a lot on your fingers if you don't take a break. When you get in the groove of crocheting, you may not want to stop, but you'll regret it later if you don't. Quick breaks to help you stretch your hands will help you to go for longer. You'll find that finger rolls help as well. There's no reason for you to experience cramping, but holding the hook for too long will do just that. Rolling your wrist will help to keep cramping away as well.

Tip #2 Posture Counts

Posture can make a difference. Even in crocheting, and you shouldn't slouch if your crocheting is going to go smoothly. This can cause pain in your back, neck, and just in general. This is just as bad as a cramp in your hand, and it'll make it where you won't want to crochet again in the future no matter how much fun you're having during your crochet session.

Tip #3 Keep a Basket

You can use a bag if you don't have a basket, but it's great to have one close by with everything that you need from yarn to hooks. You'll also want to add in a pair of scissors so that you don't constantly have to move around and find them, which could break the pattern that you get into and cause you to make mistakes. When just starting, a lot of people have it spread out all over the place, and this can lead to unneeded frustration as well.

Step #4 Keep a Slow Pace

Don't try to just keep going as fast as you can or you'll make a sloppy mistake. You don't need to get a project done too quickly, and you should always give yourself enough time to complete a project if you want it to turn out properly. If you move too fast, you're likely to miss a stitch or worse. Remember that not every yarn is easy to unravel.

Step #5 Finish Your Projects

It's important that you always try and finish your project. When you're just starting, it's easy to put a project down. It's even easier to put it down when you've made a mistake. If you've made a mistake, fake it for now. Keep going, and try to fix it as best you can. Either way, you need to finish the project so that it will help to do it for the practice. Practice really does make perfect, and crocheting is no different.

Conclusion

Crocheting is easy for beginners, but you need to stick to it. Think about projects that you can use. Always stick with simple projects, and build yourself up from there. There's nothing wrong with learning one stitch first before moving onward. You'll find that there are many crochet projects out there. You'll go from a beginner to an expert in no time.

Check the web if you want to find more free projects. There are many different websites and blogs that are dedicated to crocheting, and it's important to practice free form as well. If you are looking to make a new design, then you can play around with your own stitches. Just keep in mind that you should always write down what you're doing if you want to be able to follow the pattern later.

Using the abbreviations will save you time. Many people will keep a pen and notepad with them for when they're using free form. No matter what, just remember not to get discouraged. There's always something new in the world of crochet that you can tackle.

POBOX 16994, SD CA 92176
619-546-4949

Made in the USA
San Bernardino, CA
06 December 2017